UNTAMED

The Taming of Cambridge

_____

NIGEL EDWARDS

The Fatman Collection

This all started when I was homeless. I stayed in a homeless project in various churches and a synagogue. The volunteers there kept on telling everyone to keep tame. I was a bit odd and annoying.

I then moved into a shared house and I told one of the guys I lived with about it. He went around telling everyone on the street that I wasn't tame. He also told them I couldn't read or write.

People on the street kept taking the piss out of me, and so I decided to write this collection of poems taking the piss out of him.

Backward

The way you do it is just no good,
You are backward.
I can't relate,
You can't even communicate.

What the hell is wrong with you?
You don't have a clue.
Every word you say,
Makes me not want to stay.

It's not how it should be,
You're nothing but a future bad memory.

Bat Shit Crazy

Stupid and lazy.
When he talks about me,
I wonder if he understands reality.
Just don't know what to say,
It's the same everyday.

Talks to me like I'm an animal,
That stupid fool.
He has no respect for anyone,
It's just not cool.

He just sits there all day,
With only negative stuff to say.
Such an unimportant man,
I say be normal, you can.

But he's bat shit crazy,
Hates everything he can see.
I don't want him anywhere near me.

Been Telling Lies

Can he read and write?
Does he want a fight?
Just can't figure him out.
Want to knock him down for the count.

He keeps on lying,
I'll wait until he's crying.
What was the reason why?
Don't even try.

Cold-Blooded

Like a reptile,
Never seen him smile.
Watching telly all day,
Watching time tick away.

That man is cold-blooded,
Hope that no-one knows what he did.
Never met such a stupid man,
Whatever he says won't give a damn.

Every time he talks,
I want to walk.
Always lies,
And silly alibis.

He has no human emotion,
The way he thinks is just so slow.

Couch Potato

Might be something good on T.V tonight,
I have no life,
Don't even have a wife.
I wish I had a life.

Just sitting here all day,
Can't even get any of them hey.
Trying to think of something to say,
It always seems like the same day.

Got no friends with whom to play,
The T.V's my friend,
Come what may.

Fat and Stupid

He is so fat and stupid,
Need to tell people what he did.
Doesn't know how to keep his mouth shut,
Sounds like he lives in a hut.

All he does is he,
Want to belt him, would if I try.
Hate that man,
Want to get rid of him, anyway I can.

Fat, Lazy & Crazy

Had enough of that man,
Wish I could hit him,
And I can.

He doesn't listen to a fucking word,
There is nothing he has learned.

He keeps on telling his lies,
I want to hit him until he cries.

Got No-One To Watch T.V With

When I get out of bed, inside I feel dead.
About my day, can't think of a word to say.
Looking out the windows, there's no one I know.
Every day the same, got nothing to do again.

I haven't even got a friend, sometimes I wish this life
to end.
All day in front of the T.V, nobody with me.
Can have pie and chips, don't know how to get my
kicks.
If T.V with, this is not the life I want to live.

He Just Won't Learn

Won't listen to a word I say.
Don't want him to stay.

Want to tear his spine out.
Just won't lean,
Won't leave me alone.

Going to tear his heart out.
Get the fuck out.

Little Boy

He keeps on calling me a little boy.
Thinks he's playing with a toy.

Going to lose my temper,
Every word I can remember.

Want to tear him apart,
Going to start,
He doesn't even have a heart.

Mr. Nobody

Some people are sad,
Some people are mad.
What to say abut that twat,
He is all of that.

Everyday saying the thing,
Over and over again.
Is there nothing in your brain?

Just sitting in your room,
No job, no wife, no life.
What do you see when you look in the mirror?
Don't you want to be who you are?

Now that you're old,
Inside you're cold.
You never went far,
Nobody cares who you are.

Self Esteem

Sitting around,
Bored out of my brains.
It's always the same,
I'm going insane.

Looking out of the window,
They are people I don't know.
Don't know where to go,
What to do, I just don't know.

If I was big and strong,
And felt like I could belong.
Can't shake this sadness out of my head,
Nobody would care if I was dead.

Don't know what to do.
People treat me like I don't have a clue.

Sofa Spud

Every day the same,
Nobody knows my name.
Wish I was somebody,
Nobody wants to know me.

Can't even get a girl,
My life is hell.
I just get fatter and fatter,
I just don't matter.

I keep on going nowhere,
No-one will care.
I'm just a fat stupid couch potato,
No-one will want to know.

Stupid Fat Man

Sick of this shit,
That stupid fat old git.
Want to jump all over his head,
I wish he was dead.
Just leave me alone.
Wish we didn't live in the same home.

Stupid Man

Fat, stupid man,
Will try to communicate if I can.

He just sits there and watches T.V,
As stupid as can be.

Don't want him to be with me.
He won't leave me be,

Is not all what you can see.
Would belt him in the head,
Wish he was dead.

Not very clever,
Every word I can remember.
Just one more thing I want to say,
It shouldn't be this way.

T.V All Day

Such a useless lump of dead weight, full of hate.
He does nothing but sit there all day, with nothing
to say.
A man without a wife, a man without a life.
Just couldn't live that way, watching T.V all day.

When I listen to his stupid words,
that man doesn't understand the bees and the birds.
Just sitting in his chair all day,
How could anyone live their life that way?

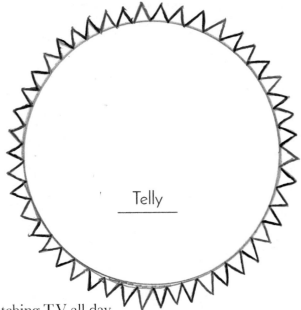

Telly

Watching T.V all day,
Making the eyes strain,
Everyday always the same.

Can think about some food to eat,
But there are no people I will meet.
Seen this film before,
I'll just sit here and watch some more.

Get up and go to bed,
Inside I feel dead.
Some sport on telly might cheer me up,
I wish I had someone to love.

Just sitting here all day,
And I'll do the same again.
No highlight to my day,
Always the same.

Might go to the shop,
Then back home.
This is where I stop,
Feeling so alone.

People ask what I've been doing,
I say not a lot.

Just going to sit here until my dying day,
I've never got anything interesting to say.

Weirdo

"Will not leave it be," is what he said to me.
Making me feel sick inside, every word a lie.
Can't understand, will toy.
To what do you do?
Will you listen to a word?
What have you learned?
One more time, don't lie, are you high?

Won't Learn

Won't learn,
Did try to explain,
Are you insane?

Don't know what to say,
Don't want you to stay.

Will listen to every word you say,
Not going to play.

Can't you feel my heart?
It will tear you apart.

Why won't you stop?
You don't know a lot.

They always say go with your gut,
If it was up to me I'd have you shot.

Won't Leave Me Alone

Feeling sad inside,
People know I have lied.
Trying to hide.
What will they do,
When they know I have lied.

Just wanted some company,
But nobody wants to be with me.
Just don't want them to ignore,
Don't know what I do this for.

All I ever get is, "leave me alone",
And no-one ever calls on the phone.

Stupid Words

His stupid words echo around my head.
I hate every word he said.
Sitting there,
letting everyone know he don't care.

There must be something I can do,
But he just doesn't have a clue.
Always telling lies and eating too many pies.
Nothing in his life but T.V
Do not want this man with me.

But the creep won't leave me alone,
Wish we didn't live in the same home.
That cheap, lousy, scumbag lives in a dream world.
It makes me sad there are people like that.
To hell with the twat.

Backwards II

Barking mad,
Sad and just bad.
As backward as you like,
Can't read or write.

I don't do a thing but watch T.V,
Nobody wants to be with me.
When I look in the mirror,
I don't like what I see.

I'm ugly as can be.
This is nothing I like about me.
I don't understand what people say.
Want to enjoy life, but just can't find a way.

The Untamed Collection

As I explained in the introduction to the Fat Man collection, this taming thing was a bit weird. What happened next was sick. People decided that some of them are untame. Things got really insane. The untame people got beaten up and everybody treated them like shit.

I don't know what happened but it got really crazy.

Cheap and Tacky

Cheap and tacky,
This taming is so wacky.
The people of Cambridge,
Don't even understand the language.

In my home town,
People need to slow down.
As I walk around,
What they say is just stupid sound.

The vile words that spew out of their mouths,
They are like sick and disturbed animals.
They keep asking who I have hit.
This taming is bullshit.

Taming

Telling me I need taming
Is an odd way of complaining.
Can't tell if they are putting it on,
Not sure where they are coming from.

Things have got so crazy,
Do these people really hate me?
Shouldn't paint people with the same brush,
But they treat me like I don't mean much.

How can this be?
Are all the untamed the same as me?
What they say is not true,
Don't they have a clue?

There has been blood shed,
And some of them are dead.
This has gone too far,
Don't even know who these people are.

Demons

They are not humans, more like demons.
A disease has spread amongst the people,
They are turning evil.

I do try to ask questions,
But all I get is lies.
Perhaps it doesn't matter,
No one cares about the why.

They can all go to hell.
I'd put them in a prison cell.
The strange order of the day,
Some tame, others untame.

I know people are not very smart,
They tame others without out any art.

It's like someone opened up pandora's box,

The demons walk the earth.
Some people don't care what life is worth.

Don't Belong

They keep on saying I should be in a cell.
That would make my life a living hell.

My name doesn't matter,
I'm just one of the untamed.
I don't mind people not knowing my name,
but this is insane.

They say I can't read or write,
and I don't know how to live my life.
I don't know what I did wrong.
Always making me feel like I don't belong.

Everywhere I Go

They hate my guts,
but they don't know me,
I think they're nuts.

Here in my home town,
They all want to put me down.
Don't want to get out of bed,
They wish I was dead.

I remember years ago,
It was not so.
But the good times are gone,
Now I feel like I don't belong.

Why are they this way?
I should be broken,
I don't even know them.

They call me untame,
without even knowing my name.
They hate me everywhere I go.
They haven't got a clue,
What did I do?

Hell

Taming has lead to bloodshed.
People are dead.
I remember when people were normal.
Was it all in my head?

What they have been doing is awful.
It's like someone cast an evil spell,
And opened the door straight to hell.
The people have gone mad, this taming is just so sad.

You don't tame people, don't they even know?
We are told to keep tame wherever we go,
From people we don't know.

This has torn people apart.
The people are not very smart.

My Home Town

The people in my home town have gone crazy,
They keep telling me to throw in the towel.
Something has gone really wrong,
People make me feel like I don't belong.

Don't know what to say, it shouldn't be this way.
Everyday I've got to listen to the stupid stuff they say.
They never think they might be doing it the
wrong way.

Now they say everyone is tame or untame,
And it doesn't matter about your name.
It's not normal, people are awful and losing the plot.
This could all be forgot.

Pork Pies

Don't know if I will grow to be old.
Don't have to listen to every word I've been told.
Sometimes people just tell pork pies.
Why do people tell lies?

I remember before everyone became tame or untame,
People called me by my name.
It feels like the world has gone insane.
I hope taming never happens again.

How can people have so much hate?
So much stupidity and lack of maturity.
Some people just don't get normality.
Or even reality.

Sick

I'm so sick of the people,
they behave like they no nothing at all.
Walking down the street,
listening to the people I meet.

They won't grow up,
I've had enough.
Listening to their stupid words,
people never learn.

Now they have decided everyone is tame and untame,
it's so insane.
I'm so sick of these stupid people,
they are so evil.

They act as if life is a T.V show,
and they're making a cameo.
They're so fake I have to remind myself,
they're actually awake.

I wish they would be swallowed up in a giant earthquake.

Can't See

Blinded by the lies,

I have no idea what you see with your eyes.
You can't see a thing,
You don't know me.

How did this madness spread?
How many people need to be dead?
Can't see the reason why,
This is all one big lie.

Back before they thought I was untame,
People would address me by my name.
What the hell is wrong with the people?
Why are they now so evil?

Just one more thing to say,
It should not be this way.

Stupid People

The people of Cambridge are the stupidest people in
the world.

World famous for their uni,
They have all gone loony.
It's just so insane,
nowadays everyone is tame or untame,
It's lame.

Don't these people have brains?
How can there be tame and untamed?
I know some people have low IQs,
Put the people of Cambridge don't have a clue.

The Untamed

People don't care abut my name,
They just call me untame.
People keep acting insane,
They all hate me now I'm untame.

They ask me who have I hit.
It's not something I do, I don't get it.
They say I should be in a cell,
I try to ask why, but they do not tell.

They want to make me cry,
I don't know why.
They are going to kick my head in,
There is no way I can win.

Trying to Communicate

I do try to listen to the words people say,
But not sure if they do it the other way.
Some people are just so simple,
They think words don't mean anything at all.

They keep on saying we need to keep tame,
Everyday it's the same.
I try to say I'm not a lion,
Are you having me on?

Some of these people are just so sick,
And intellectually weak.
Trying to communicate can be impossible,
Some people say do you want a ball?

Could put in a ponytail,
It's just as stupid as hell.
Man is not tame or untame,
It is just so lame.

Trying

Don't know how to explain,
We are not all the same.
Won't you listen to award,
Isn't there anything you have learned?

I am trying to explain that I don't feel the same.
Why do I try?
It's enough to make me cry.
I won't tell you a lie.
I don't understand why I ever try.

Untame Man

Everywhere I go people say I go on the run,
They're all so dumb.
They call me a violent criminal,
Treating me like I'm nothing at all.

Everyone treats me like a fool,
They want me to fail.
They laugh at me and say I can't read or write,
it's a bit more that just impolite.

As they pass me by,
Asking if I cry,
None of this is true,
They just don't have a clue.

I'm nothing but an untamed man,
Is this some satanic plan?
Who are the other untame men?
This needs to end, and never be done again.

What is Wrong with the People?

People have been trying to break my heart,
By saying I'm not very smart.
As I walk down the street,
It's the same with everyone I meet.

They think I'm someone I'm not,
They treat me like I don't mean a lot

What the hell is wrong with people?
They just say I'm untame,
And us untamed are all the same.

What does it even mean?
Hasn't anyone got a clue?
Don't know what to do.

Will Never Forgive

Something has poisoned the brains,
There are no tames and untames.
People need to wash that poison,
Out of their brains.

It is like they are in an hypnotic trance,
I try to reason but I have no chance.
A dark cloud has been cast over Cambridge,
They use a primitive language.

They have been doing it for far too long,
How can this happen in the town where I'm from?
I will never forgive,
These people don't deserve to live.

The Dirty Old Man Collection

The problems with the guy I was living with were never ending. Problems with people on the street continued so I moved to a different house, hoping these problems would come to an end, but the problems got worse.

I moved in with two dirty old men. One called Mello Yello, and the other I nicknamed the Goblin.

They did the same thing, they told everyone around I hit people and I couldn't read or write, and I was untame.

Things just got more and more crazy.

Deplorable

He doesn't want people to know,
Hasn't got anywhere to go.
Doesn't do a thing,
Wishes he could be unseen.

Just watches T.V all day,
Doesn't want people to know he's gay.
Sits there like a useless lump of dead weight,
Full of hate.

Deplorable and unemployable.

Says everyone needs to learn to be tame,
Does this everyday.
Such a sad lonely old man,
Has no life, has no plan.

Dirty Old Man

Just sitting there all day,
Got nothing to say.
Just sat in front of the T.v,
A man no-one wants to see.
Got nothing to look forward to,
Got nothing to do.
Pisses off everyone around,
Never has his feet on the ground.
Lives in a fantasy world,
Tells everyone won't do what he's told.

He tries to be bold, but inside he's cold

Evil Elf

That stupid little evil elf,
Acts like he is twelve.
Not a proper man,
So small he could fit in a can.
Creeps around like a bug on the ground.
Has sickness inside his head,
No-one will care when he's dead.

Evil Goblin

The old man reminds me of an evil goblin,
The sort of man who will never win.
Like some mythical monster, he won't go far.
Crying his eyeballs out, will go to hell no doubt.

Sit in front of the T.V all day, want to push him out of
the way.
That man is sick in the head, wish he was dead.

Evil

The ungodly little goblin will never win.
This way he has lived his life is a sin.
Don't know where to begin,
Such a stupid evil goblin.
I hope you burn in hell.
You should be in a cell.

Fiend

When I look into his eyes,
I don't know why he tells so many lies.
The man is a fiend,
He's not what I need.
He has sickness in his soul,
I want to bury him in a hole.
He makes me want to puke my guts up,
Doesn't understand love.
They should put him back in his cell,
Then send him straight to hell.

III
___

That old man has got a sickness inside his head,
Wish he was dead.
Just sits there all day,
Won't listen to what I say.
Should be in a cell,
Hope you go to hell.
Stupid sick old man,
As ill as the son of Sam.

In a Prison Cell

That stupid little gremlin,
I hope to tear him limb from limb.

Don't want to remember him,
My patience is running thin.

Can't hit him, feeble little goblin.
Just sits there with his pot belly, watching telly.

Really hope he burns in hell,
Should be in a prison cell.

Mello Yello

A man known by may names,
A man with no brains.

They call him Mello Yello,
Not a man I want to know.

The kids call him the evil one,
Just as stupid no-one.

They should never have let him out of his prison cell.
Hope people give him hell.

The weirdest weirdo I have ever met in my life.
With him it is always trouble and strife.

Sad, Mad and Bad

Sitting on his own,
No-one calling on the phone.
Got no friends to play with,
Got no love to give.

One of life's losses,
Ao sad and useless.
Have to listen to his stupid words everyday,
Even though he's got nothing to say.

Scared of his own shadow,
Stupid, fat and shallow.
Inside he is hollow,
Not someone I want to know.

Sick and Loathsome

Just sitting there watching your life waste way,
With nothing to say.
Just watching T.V all day everyday,
Can't give any of them hey.
Got demons inside your head,
It's like you're already dead.
Such a sick and loathsome man,
No-one will be a fan.
So fat and lazy, stupid, old and crazy.

Stupid

As stupid as a man can be,
Lives in a fantasy.
Just sits there all day watching T.V,
Do not want him to be with me.

Such a stupid liar,
Want to set him on fire.
Just a stupid old perv,
Don't know where he gets the nerve.

Aways trying to cause problems,
It never ends.
The world is better of without people like him,
The sort who will never win.

Silly Weirdo

He sits there in his dream world,
Inside he is cold.
Such a sad silly weirdo,
Not someone I want to know.

Keep on saying people need taming,
It's all need to be tame, so lame.
Can't even read a book,
Doesn't have a good look.

The world's most boring man,
Nobody will be a fan.
If I say it is black, he will say it's white,
Doesn't even have a life.

Can't get a job,
Always on his tod.

T.V Everyday

Don't understand how someone can watch T.V all
day everyday.
The old man just sits there moaning about this and
that.

How can you live your life that way,
Just sitting there everyday?
No-one ever wants him around,
For him no love can be found.

Don't want him in my life,
He should be in a cell,
I hope he goes to hell.

The Evil Little Goblin

The ungodly little goblin will never win.
The way he has lived his life is a sin.
Don't know where to begin, such a stupid evil goblin.
Hope you burn in hell, you should be in a cell.

The Evil One

The kids call him the evil one,
Just a stupid no-one.
Wants to be a mob boss,
Whatever he does it will be a loss.

Watching T.V all day,
Wasting away.

He makes me want to throw my guts up,
I've had enough.
He is a man no-one will love,
Won't end up in heaven above.

The Grim Goblin

Looks like he lives in a rubbish bin,
The dirty old grim goblin.
One of them dirty old men,
I hope never to see him again.

Just watches T.V all day,
How can a man live his life that way?
A real life boogyman,
Should have kept him in the can.

A Wasted Life

FUNERAL POEM

Once there was a man,
I don't want to remember him,
but I can.

While he walked on this earth,
He never knew what he was worth.
Dumb as a bag of rocks,
I hate him lots.

Criminal scum,
Didn't know how to have fun.
Just T.V all day everyday.
Never got a job, never meant a lot.

The Taming of Cambridge

Taming continues. Different things can effect different groups of people. Mass hysteria, mind control, old mentality. Not sure how to explain it. This has caused a lot of harm, but I am sure it is some sort of sickness.

There is no logic. People keep floating around like they do everything on autopilot. One thing I noticed is they don't do it to rich people. It has been a long time since things have been normal.

Cloven Hoof

People treat me as if I walk around with a cloven
hoof.
What they say is not the truth.
They always say who have I hit.
They sound like they mean it.

Telling me I'm going to be tamed,
Is insane.
Such a stupid use of language,
What is wrong with the people of Cambridge?

Crazy

The people of Cambridge have gone crazy,
They don't even understand why they do this to me.
When I was growing up taming was what you did to
lions,
Don't know where they get their lies from.

They treat all of the untame people as if they are the
same person,
Where are these people coming from?
They take the piss and do all they can to hurt,
Then walk off saying, "why can't we just get on?"

People have had their heads kicked in,
They act like it doesn't mean a thing.
This is just so insane, they don't even know my name.
And tomorrow they will do it again.

Every Day is the Same

Walking around, we communicate with sound.
What they say is the same everyday,
Again, again and again is driving me insane.
Now that my name is untame.

They say I should be in a cell, they can all go to hell.
Some people only get off and on, do you get where
I'm coming from?
I try to ask them why they think I'm untame,
But they don't even want to know my name.

Everyday

Have we got to do this again?
It's always the same.
Nowadays they call me vulnerable, tame,
They have all gone insane.

They harass,
And are so crass.
The people of Cambridge,
Don't seem to understand language.

They seem like they are in a hypnotic trance,
I get no answers to the questions I ask.
Hope they all go to hell,
This is making me feel unwell.

Mass Hysteria

Cambridge is suffering from mass hysteria,
Effecting everyone in the area.
People have gone insane, they talk about me,
But don't know my name.

They say I can't read or write,
Pretend they want to fight.

None of this makes any sense,
Need some sort of psychological self-defence.
They call it taming,
This needs explaining.

People Are So Fake

Walking around in a day dream,
With your head in a cloud.
Not sure if you care about the words you say,
This is not all play.

Can't believe how simple you are,
You won't go far.
You said some people are tame,
And others untame.

Don't even want to know your name,
We are not the same.
You don't even know how to communicate,
You are so fake.

People Should Keep Tame

Trying to enjoy my walk,

Don't want to listen to others talk.
Taming is not funny,
Talking to me like I'm a puppy.

They teach it in church,
They teach it in school,
Talking to me,
Like I'm a fool.

Don't they have a clue?
This is not what people should do.
Asking me who I have hit,
Some of them meaning it.

Saying that I can't read or write,
They're the ones who aren't too bright.

Stupid Madness

The taming is pathetic sadness.
It's stupid madness.
The people of Cambridge used to be normal,
Now they are just bloody awful.

They don't know how to wash the poison out of their
brains,
They have gone insane.
They have started calling people vulnerable tames,
They do this without knowing their name.

Too many people have been hit,
This is stupid bullshit.
Why can't they understand the is wrong?
They're too far gone.

The Taming of Cambridge

I can remember the words people said, not very
clever.
They are trying to make me out to be someone
I'm not,
And treat me like I don't mean a lot.

Everywhere I go, they talk to me like I'm someone
they know.
What the hell have they been doing?
How many people got beaten up?
Can't people feel love?

They never listen to a thing I say.
The same stupid shit everyday.
Have they all gone crazy?
They are so intellectually lazy.

I call it the taming of Cambridge,
We are tame or untame, this is insane.

It's Called Taming

It's called taming.

And this needs some explaining.
That's what people say.
Everyday.

Just some silly baby talk.
Not going to stay, I'll take a walk.
This has sent some to the grave.
People just don't know how to behave.

The people of Cambridge,
Need to learn language.
Too many people have been hit,
This is stupid shit.

It needs to stop, it needs to end.
I don't want it to happen to a friend.

Cambridge

The people of Cambridge,
Are the dirtiest scum you can imagine,
Don't know where to begin.
They have people tamed,
This needs to be explained.

They don't even think,
This goes on week after week.
It's been going on for so long now,
In my home town.

People are not tame or untame,
Have they all gone insane?

Won't Leave Me Be

What can I do?
You don't have a clue.
What can I say?
It shouldn't be this way.

What's the reason why?
All you do is lie.
Don't want to lose my temper,
About what you can't remember.

I'll ask you again,
My words can you recall them?
Why won't you leave me be?
You're nothing to do with me.

What's the point of calling me untame?
I do have a name.
You won't listen to a word.
Did you even go to school you fool?

How did it get to be this way?

I walk down the street,
Wondering who I will meet.
They all call me one of the untames,
We don't even know each other's names.

They try to make ne feel like shit,
And ask me who I have hit.
They don't understand,
That's not how I want to use my hand.

But they say it anyway,
This is not play.
Then they say soon I'll be in a cell,
They are making my life hell.

I ask why am I untame,
They just laugh and say it's my name.

Don't Belong

They keep on saying I should be in a cell,
Making my life a living hell.
My name doesn't matter,
Im just one of the untamed,
I don't mind people not knowing my name,
But this is insane.

They say I can't read or write,
I won't know how to live my life.
Don't know what I did wrong,
Want to make me feel like I don't belong.

Trying to Walk

This is a systematic dumbing down of the people,
They are getting evil.
They have such a limited vocabulary,
When they talk to me.

Don't know what they can see,
Saying I won't get a key.
How can two men tell each other to keep tame,
It's just so lame.

Talking about me, saying we need to keep you tame,
You don't even know my name.
Just silly baby talk,
Just trying to walk.

Wait Until You've Been Tamed

Something has poisoned their brains,
Everyday is the same.
They don't listen to a word I say,
And call me untame.

When an untame gets beaten up,
They show him no love.
They all say you got tamed,
This needs to be explained.

The taming is a disease,
Too much hate people please.

Cambridge is Cursed

Evil has spread like wildfire,
Everyone has become a liar.
People act like they can't hear a word,
I say it shouldn't be this way.

It's like they are in a hypnotic trance,
So many questions I want to ask.
There is no such thing as tame and untame people,
The only word I can think of is evil.

Cambridge has a curse,
How can it get any worse?

Something Wrong with the People

The people in my home town,

Keep on saying they throw in the towel.
They have turned into disgusting animals,
They are childish fools.

They have turned some people into untame men.
They call me one of them.
Everywhere I go,
I get disrespect from people I don't know.

Something is very wrong with the people,
They keep on asking me to go out on the pull.
Always pestering me for my attention,
With another stupid question.

All the time they lie.
I don't even think they know the reason why.

The Bully

Everyday listening to the same stupid words,
No lessons learned.
Again and again,
Everyday the same.

They say we bully,
People in my home town, as I walk around.
They don't just do this to me,
Don't know what they can see.

They treat us so called untamed,
As if we are all the same.
They need to learn man is not tame or untame,
But everyday is the same.

Paperback ISBN: 9798387516979
Hardback ISBN: 9798387517174

Published by Broken Hearted Publishing

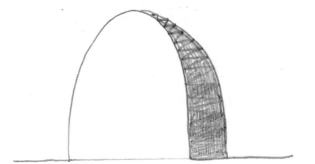

Printed in Great Britain
by Amazon